101 SILLY
Halloween JOKES
FOR KIDS

101 SILLY Halloween JOKES

FOR KIDS

Jess Kiddin

ULYSSES BOOKS
FOR YOUNG READERS

Published by:
Ulysses Books for Young Readers
an imprint of Ulysses Press
32 Court Street, Suite 2109
Brooklyn, NY 11201

ISBN: 978-1-61243-965-5
Library of Congress Control Number: 2025933936

Printed in Canada
2 4 6 8 10 9 7 5 3 1

Image credits from shutterstock.com:
cover © Ori Artiste; interior bats © KsanaGraphica;
interior graveyard © shaineast

What is a ghost's favorite dessert?

Boo-berry pie.

What does a ghost
eat with his pie?

I-scream.

What do you call a skeleton that lies around all day?

Lazy bones.

What happened to the naughty little witch at school?

She was ex-spelled.

What do you get when you cross a snowman with a vampire?

Frostbite.

What has six legs and flies?

A witch giving
her cat a ride.

Where did the vampire open his savings account?

At a blood bank.

Why did the ghost go to the doctor?

To get his boo-ster shot.

How do ghosts earn points in a football game?

They kick the ball between the ghoul posts.

Where do mummies go for a swim?

The Dead Sea

What do you call a witch with one leg?

I-lean.

What was the little witch's favorite subject at school?

Spelling.

What happened at the vampires' race?

They finished neck
and neck.

Why do cemeteries have fences?

Because people are dying to get in.

What happened when two vampires met?

It was love at first bite.

What do little vampires learn in kindergarten?

The alpha-bat.

Why did the skeleton miss the party?

He had no-body to go with.

What kind of mistakes do ghosts make?

Boo boos.

What's a ghoul's favorite game?

Hide-and-go-shriek.

What does a vampire take for a bad cold?

Coffin drops.

What does a near-sighted ghost need?

Spook-tacles.

What is a monster's favorite game?

Swallow the leader.

What do you call a haunted chicken?

A poultry-geist.

What is a ghost's favorite toy?

A boo-merang.

What did the bat say to the witch's hat?

You go on a-head, and I'll hang around for a while.

What is a vampire's favorite fruit?

A neck-tarine.

What is a vampire's second favorite fruit?

A blood orange.

What two famous places did the monster visit on his vacation?

The Vampire State Building and Count Rushmore.

What does a werewolf put on before he goes to the beach?

Moon tan lotion.

Where did the ghost get its hair done?

At the boo-ty shop.

What's a monster's favorite play?

Romeo and Ghouliet.

What instrument do skeletons play?

Trombone.

Who protects
the shores where
spirits live?

The ghost guard.

Who won the monster beauty contest?

No one.

What do you call a witch who lives at the beach?

A sand-witch.

What happens if a big, hairy monster sits in front of you at the movies?

You miss most of the film.

What do ghosts eat for dinner?

Ghoulash.

Where do spirits mail their letters?

At the ghost office.

What do you call zombies in a belfry?

Dead ringers.

What kind of tests do they give in witch school?

Hex-aminations.

Where do ghosts go on vacation?

Mali-boo.

What kind of music do mummies like?

Wrap music.

Why do skeletons
hate winter?

**Because the wind goes
right through them.**

What do you call two witches who share an apartment?

Broom-mates.

What is Dracula's favorite sport?

Bat-minton.

How many vampires does it take to change a light bulb?

None—vampires like the dark.

Why did the monster eat a light bulb?

He wanted a light snack.

What is a monster's favorite drink?

Demonade.

What did the mother ghost say to her kids in the car?

Fasten your sheet belts.

Why doesn't Dracula have any friends?

He's just a pain
in the neck.

Why are ghosts bad at lying?

You can see right through them.

What do you get if you cross Dracula with a snail?

The world's slowest vampire.

How do you fix a jack-o'-lantern?

With a pumpkin patch.

What do you get if a monster sits on your piano?

Flat notes.

Why don't witches ride their brooms when they're angry?

They're afraid of flying off the handle.

What do you get if you cross a spider and an elephant?

I'm not sure, but if you see one walking across the ceiling, run!

When does Count Dracula relax at work?

During his coffin break.

Why do witches fly on broomsticks?

Vacuum cleaners are too expensive.

What do you get when you cross a black cat with a lemon?

A sour-puss.

When do ghosts usually appear?

Just before someone screams.

What is the scariest ride at the carnival?

The roller ghoster.

What do you get if you cross a monster with peanut butter?

A monster that sticks to the roof of your mouth.

What's black, white, and orange and waddles?

A penguin carrying a jack-o'-lantern.

How do you make a skeleton laugh?

Tickle his funny bone.

What do you call a stupid skeleton?

Bonehead.

What time is it when a monster sits on your car?

Time to get a new car.

What is a vampire's least favorite food?

Stake.

How are vampires
like false teeth?

They come out at night.

What kind of witch can jump higher than a bus?

Any kind—buses can't jump.

What's a vampire's favorite animal?

A giraffe.

What runs around a cemetery but doesn't move?

A fence.

How do you make
a witch float?

**You take two scoops of
ice cream, a glass of root
beer, and one witch...**

What breed of dog does Dracula have?

A blood hound.

What's big and ugly and bounces?

A monster on a pogo stick.

**Did you hear about
the monster that
lost his left arm and
leg in a car crash?**

He's all right now.

Why did the vampire give his girlfriend a blood test?

To see if she was his type.

What do you get if you cross a dinosaur with a witch?

A Tyrannosaurus hex.

What is scarier than an angry witch?

Two angry witches.

What does a monster eat in a restaurant?

The waiter.

Did you hear about the monster with five legs?

His pants fit him like a glove.

What do goblins drink when they're hot and thirsty?

Ghoul-aid.

What goes cackle, cackle, bonk?

A witch laughing
her head off.

What did the bird say on Halloween?

Trick or tweet!

What time is it when ghosts haunt your house?

Time to get a new house.

Why don't skeletons play music in church?

They have no organs.

What is the tallest building in Transylvania?

The Vampire State Building.

What kind of vehicle does Dr. Frankenstein drive?

A Monster Truck.

What is evil, ugly, and keeps the neighbors awake?

A witch with a drum kit.

How do you keep an ugly monster in suspense?

I'll tell you tomorrow.

What's big and hairy and goes beep beep?

A monster in a traffic jam.

What do little ghosts say when they run out of Halloween candy?

Boo hoo.

Who sells cookies to monsters?

The ghoul scouts.

Who do vampires invite to family reunions?

Blood relations.

Why did the monster knit herself three socks?

Because she grew another foot.

What is big, slimy, ugly, and turns blue?

A monster holding its breath.

What is scary and loves to dance?

The boogieman.

What is a sea monster's favorite dish?

Fish and ships.

What do you get if you cross a cocker spaniel, a poodle, and a ghost?

A cocker-poodle-boo.

What happened to the monster that took the five o'clock train home?

He had to give it back.

What do you get if you remove the insides of a hot dog?

A hollow weenie.

What does a skeleton order at a restaurant?

Spare ribs.

What's Dracula's favorite flavor of ice cream?

Vein-illa.

What did the mommy vampire say to the baby vampire?

"You're driving me batty!"

What did the monster say when he saw a train full of passengers?

Oh, good! A chew chew train!

Why are black cats such good singers?

They're very mewsical.

What is the best way to talk to Dracula?

Long distance.

Add Your Own Jokes!